MW00717297

101 USES FOR A YORKIE

© 2015 Willow Creek Press

All Rights Reserved. No part of this book may be reproduced or transmitted in any form by any means, electronic or mechanical, including photocopying, recording, or by any information storage and retrieval system, without written permission from the publisher.

Published by Willow Creek Press, Inc.
P.O. Box 147, Minocqua, Wisconsin 54548

p5 © Iakov Filimonov/istockphoto.com; p9 (right) © AlexArtPhoto/istockphoto.com; p10 © SuperStock/agefotostock.com;
p13 (right) © Sabine Schrhagel/imageBROKER/agefotostock.com; p14 © Missing35mm/istockphoto.com;
p15 © Juniors Bildarchiv/agefotostock.com; p16 © Savushkin/istockphoto.com; p17 © H. Schmidt-Roeger/agefotostock.com;
p18 © kuban_girl/istockphoto.com; p19 © Juniors Bildarchiv/agefotostock.com; p20 © Lisa Thornberg/istockphoto.com;
p21 © Ruth Rose Photography/istockphoto.com; p22 © dlewis33/istockphoto.com;
p23 © Tierfotoagentur/Ramona Richter/agefotostock.com; p25 © sshepard/istockphoto.com;
p26 © Brinkmann Tierfoto/agefotostock.com; p27 © Tierfotoagentur/Alexa P./agefotostock.com;
p28 (left) © Kharichkina/istockphoto.com; (right) © cynoclub/istockphoto.com; p30 © irabassi/istockphoto.com;
p33 © SuperStock/agefotostock.com; p35 © Jim Vallee/istockphoto.com; p37 © RFcompany/agefotostock.com;
p38 © Lisa Thornberg/istockphoto.com; p41 © H. Schmidt-Roeger/agefotostock.com; p42 © MIXA/agefotostock.com;
p46 © Lisa Thornberg/istockphoto.com; p47 © Julie and Vic Pigula/istockphoto.com; p48 © Lisa Thornberg/istockphoto.com;
p51 © oleghz/istockphoto.com; p53 © kuban_girl/istockphoto.com; p54 (left) © Art Wolfe Stock/agefotostock.com;
(right) © FLPA/Angela Hampton/gefotostock.com; p57 © Caroline Brinkmann/imageBROKER/agefotostock.com;
p58 © Zoonar/Peter Meurer/agefotostock.com; p59 © Lisa Thornberg/istockphoto.com; p60 © CSP_kadmy/agefotostock.com;
p61 © Juniors Bildarchiv/agefotostock.com; p62 © Iztok Noc/istockphoto.com; p63 © Digoarpi/istockphoto.com;
p64 © jtyler/istockphoto.com; p65 © Lisa Thornberg/istockphoto.com; p66 © Lisa Thornberg/istockphoto.com;
p67 © Foto-front/istockphoto.com; p68 © Iakov Filimonov/istockphoto.com; p70 © Gonzalo Azumendi/agefotostock.com;
p71 © kuban_girl/istockphoto.com; p72 © Juniors Bildarchiv/agefotostock.com; p73 © belchonock/istockphoto.com;
p74 © Lisa Thornberg/istockphoto.com; p75 © Tierfotoagentur/A. Geier/agefotostock.com;
p76 © Juniors Bildarchiv/agefotostock.com; p78 © Bernd Brinkmann/agefotostock.com; p80 © Lisa Thornberg/istockphoto.com;
p84 © Agatalina/istockphoto.com; p88 © Lisa Thornberg/istockphoto.com; p90 © Jose Luis Pelaez Inc./agefotostock.com;
p94 © Jarrycz/istockphoto.com;

Design: Donnie Rubo
Printed in China

101 USES FOR A YORKIE

WILLOW CREEK PRESS

Spy

Snuggle Buddy

Lunch Date

Laundry Helper

Scholar

Tutor

Bookworm

Fabric Softener

Skateboarder

Escort

Lawn Mower

Rock Climber

Hiking Guide

Groundskeeper

Backseat Driver

Personal Shopper

Confidant

Garden Gnome

Security Alarm

Bed Warmer

Q-tip

Moist Towelette

Seat Warmer

Footrest

Kitchen Helper

Playmate

Hugger

Kisser

Valentine

Neighborhood Watch

Bookends

Babysitter

Sous Chef

Nanny

Washcloth

Patient

Centerfold

Diva

Fashion Accessory

Food Critic

Dishwasher

Present

Santa's Elf

Stocking-stuffer

Royalty

Trendsetter

Swimsuit Model

Beach Bum

Clown

Welcoming Committee

Lookout

GPS

Musician

Wrestler

Ballerina

Copilot

Herder

Blanket

Dreamcatcher

Couch Potato

Logger

Comedian

Alarm Clock

Bathroom Cleaner

High Jumper

Personal Trainer

Medalist

Botanist

Facebook Friend

Cobbler

Fashionista

Roommate

Doorman

Furever Friends

Artist

Goalie

Pedometer

Retriever

Stuffed Animal

Measuring Stick

Long-Distance Runner

Sprinter

Hurdler

Party Planner

Hairdresser

Lifeguard

Aerobics Instructor

Stowaway

Zen master

Gardener

Florist

Romantic

Flirt

Editor

I.T. Support

Doctor

Accountant

Contractor

Leaf rake

Trailblazer

Snowplow